Hearstrings and Reflections

By: Breuna Walker

Preface

Welcome to ***Heartstrings and Reflections***. This collection is a glimpse into my own journey—a journey through the highs and lows of self-discovery and healing. These poems are more than just words on a page; these are pieces of my heart, crafted to share the moments of pain, joy, love, and loss.

I began writing poems during a challenging time in my life, marked by a layoff. These events pushed me to explore and express my emotions in a new and creative way. What started as a way to cope with these changes, soon evolved into a deeper exploration of my own heart and experiences.

The book is divided into two sections, each capturing a unique aspect of this journey:

Section 1: Self-Discovery and Self-Love:

This section dives into the process of uncovering who we are beneath the surface. It's about embracing our true selves, learning to love ourselves despite our imperfections, and navigating the twists and turns of personal growth. These poems are meant to be a mirror for anyone who's ever questioned their worth or sought to find their own path during their journey.

Section 2: Reflections on Loss and Guidance:

Here, we explore losses and the wisdom that comes from them. It's about reflecting on what we've endured, finding guidance through those times, and seeking renewal. These verses aim to offer solace and insight to those who are going through their own experiences of heartache and seeking a way to move forward.

As you read through these pages, I hope you will find a bit of yourself in my stories or can relate to something. My goal is to create a space where you can see your own heartstrings, resonating alongside mine.

Thank you for joining me on this journey. I'm excited for you to explore these poems and find your own reflections within them.

Acknowledgments

I would like to extend my deepest love and gratitude to my family and friends for their unwavering support and encouragement throughout this journey.

Special thanks to my parents, Celeste and Joe, for their constant love, support, and belief in me. You have raised me to be the person I am today, instilling in me the values of resilience, compassion, empathy, and determination.

To my aunt, Vicki, my nana, Lillie, and my granny, Genett, your love, wisdom, and strength have been a guiding light in my life.

Kalan and Anthony, thank you for being great and true friends to me, and for being my critics during this process.

Thank you to my "Heartache to Healing" group on Facebook for providing a safe space and community for others. Your support has been so wonderful and touching. Scan the QR code to join the group and connect with others on the path from heartache to healing:

And to my cousin, Tetra Tyes, for the beautiful cover and back art. Your talent and creativity have brought my vision to life. The link to her Facebook is below. She has her work on here, and a link to her website in her bio.

Facebook: https://www.facebook.com/tetra.tyes

Table of Contents

Section 1: Self-Discovery and Self-Love

A Portrait of Self Love 1

Unmasking The Circus...2-3

Life of Luxury...4

The Art of Letting Go..5

Dear Inner Child..6-7

Dreaming of Love...8-9

Overjoyed..10

Rescue Me...11

Blossoming Resilience..12

Nostalgic Daydreams..13

Outcast's Hope...14

Section 2: Reflections on Loss and Guidance

Family Reunion 16

The Warmth They Left Behind 17

Layoff..18

Endless Night...19

The Storm 20-21

Dancing with the Enemy..22

Blade of Illusions 23

Heartache to Healing..24

An Epistle to My Inner Self 25

Brilliantly Guided...26-27

God's Embrace 28

Section 1: Self-Discovery and Self-Love

A Portrait of Self-Love

I love everything my creator made on me,

And the way I've grown into who I'm meant to be.

High cheekbones and big cheeks, a smile so wide,

Big, round eyes that sparkle with pride.

Ears, lips, and a nose so small,

Kinky hair, caramel skin, both standing tall.

A light scar above my brow, a mark of my own place.

Thick eyebrows and small beauty marks that frame,

Every feature tells a story with no shame.

Unmasking the Circus

I'm so glad that I left people alone, that no longer serve a purpose,

And that I'm no longer part of the circus.

I've let people play in my face and disregard my boundaries,

Along with doing a bunch more clownery.

I had to wipe the clown makeup off my face,

Clearing the stage by putting people in their place.

People took me as a joke,

And I had to make them choke—

Choke on the hurt they inflicted,

And the bitter truth of their loss.

Never again will I see the potential in people,

And deal with anyone evil.

I feel like a bird that's burst from its cage, wings spread wide,

Embracing the sky, fueled by a fierce, fiery pride.

Now I reclaim my focus, no longer weighed down,

By anger and resentment, I cast them out.

With tears and a heart set free,

I turn to myself and see what I want to be.

The past fades away, as I arise anew,

Embracing my path, with a vision true.

Life of Luxury

I think I deserve the world,

To treat myself to diamonds and pearls.

Take me on a luxurious shopping spree,

Where we get lost in cashmere and be free.

I want to dine on the finest cuisine,

In a setting that's so serene.

Travel to places exotic and grand,

And feel the warm, golden sun on my gentle hand.

From lavish dreams to days so bright,

I've crafted a life with pure delight.

Now it's time to revel in all I've sought,

To cherish each treasure that I've bought.

With confidence, I claim what's due,

A life of luxury, for me and you.

The Art of Letting Go

Sometimes you have to let go—

Let go of people that aren't good for you,

And things that no longer serve any purpose, too.

It won't be easy,

But over time, it becomes a breeze.

If you don't let go, it takes a toll,

On your mental and physical health.

Like storm clouds burdened with grief,

Causing you so much pain.

It's pain that echoes like a distant thunder,

Lingering in the stillness, where memories murmur.

Stuck in an infinite cycle,

Often leaving you in denial.

The cycle sucks the life from you,

Making everything seem untrue.

Act now before it's too late,

Seize the moment, don't procrastinate.

Find your peace and celebrate.

Dear Inner Child

I hate that you were hard on yourself,

Neglecting the care of your mental health.

You fought so many battles alone,

When you didn't have to do it on your own.

You always put others' feelings first,

Which made your own pain much worse.

You blocked out memories, pushing them away,

Avoiding the hurt they'd bring today.

I hate that you believed the cruel lies,

When they said you were ugly in their eyes.

I wish you would have known how lovely you are,

And that you're a shining star.

Despite all you faced, you stayed kind,

Ensuring that no one was left behind.

Dear Inner Child

I wish I could hug you, instill confidence, anew,

You were such a bright soul with a pure heart, it's true.

With the intelligence of a genius, so clear,

I'm proud of the adult you've become, my dear.

It took a lot of work to become confident in yourself,

And now, your strength and wisdom are truly felt.

Dreaming of Love

I yearn for a love so gentle and sweet,

A love that sweeps me right off my feet.

A love that lingers through sleepless nights,

And shines within an enduring light.

I dream of a love from a fairy tale,

Not one that leaves me feeling frail.

A love where our eyes intertwine,

A bond that will stand the test of time.

I crave a romance, tender and grand,

To share a slow and heartfelt dance.

With soft touches under the moonlit skies,

And 90's R&B as our lullabies.

A love that heals, both strong and kind,

With conversations that deeply bind.

We'll share our stories, secrets so true,

The perfect vision crafted for me and you.

We'll dig deep in each other's souls,

Helping each other become whole.

Together, we'll break generational curses, ending pain.

No longer will we bury hurt in the dirt,

As a strong team, we'll rise above and conquer the world, hand in hand.

Overjoyed

I finally found my smile again,

No longer hiding and pretending.

No more charades or hidden disguise,

My true self flourishes, no compromise.

It took so much healing, time to mend,

A journey within, that won't end.

Inner peace, once out of reach,

Now fills my soul with soothing ease.

I'm doing the things I once used to do,

Rediscovering passions, embracing the new.

Like a butterfly, flying high in the sky,

I embrace new heights as I continue to rise.

Rescue Me

I know someday, he'll arrive,

To lift me from the shadows where I've strived.

He'll guide me through, and help me thrive,

And in his embrace, I'll find peace that survives.

With his arms around me, so secure and kind,

He'll leave the wounds left behind with time.

In his presence, I'll feel truly safe,

Reclaiming joy, like a child that plays.

Our love will dance on cloud nine,

Beneath a sky, where our dreams intertwine.

He'll be my rock, steady and true,

Our bond grows stronger with each passing view.

I await the dawn of our shared fate,

To see our story unfold, intricate and great.

With every sunrise, our love will renew,

Crafting a life, vibrant and true.

Blossoming Resilience

I'm so proud of the person you've become,

Your strength shines through when battles come.

Even when the world seems disarrayed,

You stand tall, showing strength displayed.

Through each challenge, day and night,

You tackle the trials with courage in sight.

Despite the harshness others may show,

Your compassion remains a shiny glow.

Though the world might not always be kind,

You rise above, with peace of mind.

Forgiveness guides you; anger you disdain,

A true sweetheart, where love remains.

Keep your head high and dreams in sight,

Continue to soar, with your spirit's light.

Nostalgic Daydream

Take me back to the good old days,

Where I didn't have a care in the world.

And I, a child, wandering with ease,

Breathing the sweet, nostalgic breeze.

My desktop and consoles, portals of delight,

Barbies and their houses, a room full of toys in sight.

Singing on my karaoke machine, recording each tune,

Lost in the melodies from morning to afternoon.

Watching music videos, dancing with flair,

My cousin and I lost in the rhythms we shared.

Getting lost in books, adventures so grand,

Traveling to far-off places, a book in my hand.

Now those moments seem so far away,

A cherished past where I wished to stay.

Though time has moved on and I've grown so fast,

Those moments linger, a love that will last.

Outcast's Hope

I've always felt like an outcast,

Praying each day this feeling won't last.

Trapped inside of a box, I try to break free,

While everyone watches, ignoring me.

My interests so different, set me apart,

A unique rhythm beats within my heart.

While others revel in the ordinary and plain,

I seek the extraordinary, breaking the chain.

The way I carry myself, distinct and rare,

A lonely soul wondering, searching for where—

I truly belong, where I can be,

Not an outcast, but authentically me.

Although the world can be evil and cold,

I hold onto hope that my story will unfold.

One day, I will find my tribe,

And not worry about having to hide.

Section 2: Reflections on Loss and Guidance

Family Reunion

Family isn't how it used to be,

Our closeness faded like a distant plea.

The ones who kept the glue together,

Are in our hearts, now and forever.

A void that time can't mend.

A longing for bonds that we can't pretend.

The older members feel the rift's lament,

Their frowns, a sign of deep discontent.

Wishing that family would come around,

And longing for a solid, common ground.

Family get-togethers, now rare and incomplete,

Empty chairs and silence, where laughter used to meet.

Yet through the whispers, a faint hope persists,

That love's enduring thread might yet re-exist.

I miss the days where our family felt more complete,

When every gathering was a cherished retreat.

One day, hopefully, we'll find our way back,

To the warmth of togetherness, we once had.

The Warmth They Left Behind

I hope I make my lost loved ones proud,

With cheers roaring clear and loud.

I know that they're guiding me,

Through every challenge, every victory.

Their wisdom and love are so warm,

In their embrace, no harm can form.

They turn my pain into strength and power,

Their support unwavering, hour by hour.

They hear my cries and feel my distress,

Their gentle spirits bring comfort and rest.

I cherish their love so much,

Yet I grieve that they couldn't see me grow up.

Though they're gone, their love still guides me,

Their legacy blooms in who I've become.

Layoff

Here I am; I've just lost my job,

And all I can do is uncontrollably sob.

Why did this happen to me? How could it be?

Just as I was getting back on my feet.

I feel like I'm stuck in a tiny cell,

With no escape from the pits of hell.

My pain bursts forth in a thunderous shout.

I have a lot on my plate,

And all I can do is nervously shake.

It feels like life's playing me as a joke,

And all I have is a mustard seed of hope.

The road ahead looks curvy,

And I can't help but hurry.

In this moment, I pause and relax,

And try my hardest to stay on track.

Endless Night

I can't escape the grip of my deep distress,

My mind, a prison, with no light to confess.

In dreams, monstrous figures chase me relentlessly.

Their roars radiate my fears, as I run hopelessly.

I also have visions of free-falling endlessly,

Plunging through a void that mirrors my own misery.

Signs that I need to face my problems head-on,

But the path is unclear, and I feel so withdrawn.

As I search for light in this endless night,

The shadows whisper secrets I can't fight.

In the dark, a raspy voice calls my name in terror.

Will I face the darkness, or be lost forever?

The Storm

I really hate how things ended up this way,

I'm trying to take things day by day.

My mind is cloudy, and I've grown rowdy.

I feel betrayed, and I most definitely feel played.

It feels like my heart has been shattered into many pieces,

And a part of me is missing.

My world feels completely upside down,

And all I can do is frown.

Dark clouds are looming over me,

Make me long to flee.

They're filled with anger, sadness, and fears,

And are also filled with tears.

A fear to love again and let anyone in my space.

A fear of going through the same pain,

And once again, being left in the rain.

The Storm

The scars run deep, stealing my peace.

In this cloudy storm, I seek to find,

A place of quiet and peace of mind.

Dancing with the Enemy

Like a tsunami tearing through a calm ocean,

You left me in a sea of lost dreams and empty promises.

I tangoed with shadows in a masquerade of lies,

Each step, a deceptive gancho[1] with the enemy's wicked embrace.

Thinking about it makes my body mildly ache,

A lingering pain, I cannot seem to shake.

I poured time and care into your fractured soul,

Always bandaging your wounds, while losing sight of my own role.

Now, I tread cautiously through memories,

Scared and bruised,

A loud reminder of the love and trust I once abused.

---

[1] Gancho - A dance move in tango where one partner hooks their leg around the other partner's leg.

Blade of Illusions

Rest in peace to the person I thought you once were;

That version of you is now a blur.

I fell in love with a façade,

Which slowly turned into a blade—

A blade of deceit,

That left my heart and mind incomplete.

It cut deep, and over time,

I've been healing from the wounds it left behind.

I'm still wiping up the blood,

Cleaning up the mess as I mend and rebuild.

Rest in peace to what's left behind,

For in the ashes, new strength I find.

The blood I wiped away, a story told,

In the healing light, my heart turns cold.

From the remnants of pain, new life will grow,

A testament to the strength I now know.

From Heartache to Healing

I'm on the journey of healing,

For my emotional and physical well-being.

I've been through a lot,

To where I feel like I'm all that I've got.

From trauma, grief, failed relationships, and trust issues,

I'm learning to navigate these complex tissues.

With every step forward, I feel stronger,

Determined to find peace, no matter how much longer.

I've discovered that healing isn't a straight line;

It's a twisted path, taking its sweet time.

Through self-love and patience, I start to see

A glimpse of the person I once used to be.

Surrounded by hope, embracing the light,

I'm reclaiming my power, preparing to fight.

With each day, I rise from pain,

Ready to live, love, and dream again.

An Epistle to My Inner Self

To my inner self,

Your growth has truly amazed me,

No longer bound by hurt, anger, or low self-esteem.

You've learned to love yourself,

And forgive those who've hurt you.

You've also learned to set healthy boundaries, too.

You stand up for yourself,

Refusing to back down,

Never stooping low, wearing your crown.

Confident and capable, you're ready for the quest,

Determined to conquer, always giving your best.

Keep blossoming and evolving, like a radiant sunflower's grace,

For in your journey, you've found a heartfelt place.

Brilliantly Guided

They used to be the sweetest soul,

With a love that made others whole.

But pain, like shadows crept inside,

And their trust slowly died.

They build their walls, a fortress high,

To shield their heart and hide their cries.

They ran away to escape the pain,

To forget the memories that chain.

With each drop, carried a wound so deep,

A storm of hurt, so steep.

Their disappointment in others continued to grow,

Yet they offered their hand, through their sorrow.

Though their heart became a guarded space,

They learned to give with measured grace.

Their circle narrowed, trust was strained,

Their heart shielded yet love remained.

Brilliantly Guided

Though they held back, their care still showed,

In every gesture, their seeds were grown.

Their guarded ways a shield and guide,

Yet their warmth couldn't be denied.

With every cautious step they took,

They wrote new chapters, each a book.

In learning to protect their soul,

They found a way to still be whole.

The warmest soul, with a tempered heart,

Navigated pain, a work of art.

Their trust may falter, yet they strive,

To keep the spark of love alive.

God's Embrace

God, I'm really trying my best,

But I need you to help me find rest.

I'm trying to do so much alone,

And I'm just so tired of having to be strong.

Defeated, with embers of anger inside,

I can no longer run away from my problems or hide.

Life's trials have come in waves, so strong and gray,

All I can do is kneel and pray.

Pray for days where burdens fade,

And my spirit finds the calm I've sought.

Praying for a calm river to wash away the storm.

To cool the fires that burn within,

And let the serenity gently begin.

Connect with Me

Thank you for reading! If you enjoyed this chapbook, I'd love to stay in touch with you.

Follow me on social media:
Instagram: @_QueenBreuna and @BresPositiveSpace

X: @SincerelyBreuna

Facebook: Breuna Walker or https://www.facebook.com/SincerelyBreuna/

Feel free to reach out or share your thoughts!